MW00929825

CPSIA information can be obtained
at www.ICGtesting.com
Printed in the USA
FSHW021255060919
61782FS

9 781722 829254